FORGED
A GUIDE TO BECOMING A BLACKSMITH

It is vain to do with more, what can be done with less
- William of Occam

Hoffman shop, spring 2009

© 2017 Liam Hoffman
All rights reserved.
ISBN: 1546602135
ISBN 13: 9781546602132

Contents

Preface

9

Planning your workspace

13

Essential tools

23

Luxury Tools

63

Budget Shop Formulas

91

Safety

95

How to teach yourself

123

Afterword

139

Appendix

147

Work Journal

148

RESOURCES FOR BEGINNERS

149

ONLINE MATERIAL AND TOOL SUPPLIERS

152

DEFINITIONS

154

BOOK REFERENCES

158

ABOUT THE AUTHOR

160

Acknowledgements

Without the support and guidance from the following people and organizations, I would not be doing what I'm doing today.

Mom and Dad, you've both continually given me the support and free reign to develop my skills and business over the last eight years. I'm sure this wasn't the easiest at times, but, hey, I turned out all right. Thank you, Jason Lonon. You tried to avoid giving me your tutelage at first when I was a thirteen-year-old boy, but when I unknowingly and coincidentally showed up in your welding course three years later, you knew you couldn't avoid it. Thanks for giving me a guiding hand that I could trust in blacksmithing and general shop talk. Having a well-rounded blacksmith whom I can bounce ideas off of has been invaluable. Brian Witherspoon, no matter how gruff you are on the outside, you were one of the people most willing to help me. Thank you for dedicating your time in the evenings while I was in high school. You showed me how to photograph my work, showed me what my work should and shouldn't be, and supported my growing business. Lastly, thank you to everyone at the North Carolina Custom Knife Makers Guild for showing a scrawny sixteen-year-old what you know. Mom and Dad, Jason, Brian, and the

NCCKMG, you all have had a profound impact on my life. Thank you.

PREFACE

In 2016, at age nineteen, I won the nationally televised "Forged in Fire" competition against an ABS Master Bladesmith in Brooklyn, New York, hosted by the History Channel. Although very young—the youngest smith ever to win the competition—I had benefited from a six-year journey into the craft of blacksmithing that began at age thirteen, when I gathered together a few household utensils and began to pound on a piece of aluminum. This book distills the essential features of that six-year learning curve in the hope that it will help other beginners like you to make a similar journey.

Along that way, I hope you will discover, as I have, the joy and sense of accomplishment that comes from forming materials into useful and beautiful shapes, mastering an ancient technology, and interacting and competing with master smiths (directly and via the Internet) who are very willing to help beginners by sharing their expertise.

This book does not claim to be the only resource that you will need in order to successfully begin blacksmithing. What it does is point out solutions to stumbling blocks that confront beginners, thereby saving time, money, and much frustration. There are four main areas in which obstacles are likely to be encountered: the workspace where you will learn the craft, the tools that you will acquire or build to work on your projects, the gear and equipment modifications that are required for you to engage in blacksmithing in a safe and healthful manner, and the way in which you learn from yourself and others as your skills and goals evolve. The first two sections of this book (on workplace and tools) are aimed at those who don't want to invest in a large shop equipped with expensive tools in order to get their first taste of forging. The good news is that you don't have to. I will explain how you can get started with household items gathered in one evening. However, spending a total of $300 to $3,000 is enough to provide a decent setup right from the start.

A section of this book is reserved for discussion about each of these four topics, followed by an afterword, in which I will articulate why I think blacksmithing has experienced growing popularity among enthusiasts and millennials who are seeking ways to enrich their lives and surmount the suffocating impact of our throwaway, high-tech-driven consumer culture.

Photos of my winning Kora sword

Planning your workspace

How much and what kind of space is needed to set up and work in your low-budget blacksmithing shop? One hundred square feet is plenty, and I wouldn't recommend anything more at first. In fact, even if you can afford to spend more, I *do not* recommend doing so. Starting blacksmithing in a seemingly cramped and uncomfortable space and using minimal and/or crude tools is a better way to nurture the skills you need to become successful. The workarounds that such a situation demands become an important part of your learning curve, a learning curve that is denied to those who start with a premium workplace and high-end equipment.

Why is this so? First, a small workspace enforces efficiency, and efficiency while working at the forge is vital. For example, the placement of your tools greatly affects how well and how quickly you work. An overly large workspace will tempt you to scatter your tools at distances that impair your ability to work quickly, efficiently, and effectively. As you'll soon learn, you have a very limited window of time once your steel exits the forge. Getting to the tongs, hammer, and anvil quickly is important. Have your anvil no more than two paces from your forge when starting out. *Place tools nearby in the order in which you will need to use them.* For instance, if you're about to pull a piece of hot steel out of the fire, place your tongs right next to or below your forge for easy access. Rest your hammer on your anvil or beside it for a quick grab. Setting up your tools for easy and efficient work will pay off in less time spent at the forge and higher-quality work.

Grinding station

Secondly, "big boy" tools will mostly benefit accomplished smiths who have well-established skills and who are focused on productivity and efficiency. Such tools only magnify mistakes. For example, experienced smiths already understand how a high-end $4,000–$7,000 hydraulic press works, so the equipment replaces muscle power and improves efficiency. But when a beginner buys such equipment and does not possess the underlying experience, he or she is in effect cheating on the learning process by buying skills instead of building them organically from the ground up. As one example, making Damascus steel without a power hammer or a press will provide you with a far greater understanding of how forging Damascus steel works. Learning grows from understanding *how to fail* and understanding *how things don't work* as well as from their opposites. The student who has been given all the answers without experiencing failure gains no true knowledge. More on this later. It is a very human temptation to purchase more gear to solve a problem.

Third, this approach encourages creativity, especially when you commit right away to accomplishing a simple objective. As the old adage goes, "Necessity is the mother of invention," so by committing early on to a straightforward project and purposely putting yourself in a position where a lack of extensive equipment forces you to come up with workarounds, you will force yourself to be creative in order to get the job done. Start something immediately and figure out the kinks as you go. As Mick Jagger said, "You can't always get what you want, but if you try sometimes, well, you might find you get what you need."

Fourth, and perhaps most important, a small and very simple workspace gives you a chance to start blacksmithing right away—in fact, right now! If you have a large enough backyard (and friendly neighbors), you can set up a fire pit and a lean-to shed or tent pretty much like the picture below. Although that setup might need to be replaced after a month or so, that early experience will teach you a lot about what a

Hoffman shop, spring 2010

more permanent workspace should be planned to accomplish.

Even though final shop plans will inevitably change as they respond to differing goals in terms of the quantity and quality of the items produced in them, the plan of the start-up shop should be relatively the same for all beginners. For instance, when I know that my ultimate goal is to make one knife a month, then my final shop plan will retain a relatively small footprint, reducing costs and increasing efficiency.

Entrance to the Hoffman shop

270-square-foot shop

In contrast, if my goal is to make two hundred axes a month, then I'll need a far larger shop with more equipment. This much should be obvious. Although the size of a shop (its square footage) does relate to the *volume* of products that can be produced in it, it does not relate as rigidly to the shop's *dollar revenues*. For example, although a three-hundred-square-foot shop cannot easily turn out product in high volume, it can turn out a small but steady stream of $1,000 to $10,000 knives, supporting a six-figure income (assuming the smith has the skills and reputation to justify such a high price point). The small shop (about one hundred to three hundred square feet) is all that is required for forging simple wall hooks or small fabrication projects. As discussed in the preface, workshop size and environment underlie the quality of skills that can be acquired over time (your learning curve). A small, efficient space helps you to get off to the right start in order to build your skills for the long run.

It's OK if you don't know what your one-year, five-year, or ten-year blacksmithing goals are. You can figure these things out as you go. It is helpful, but not essential, to have a basic idea of what you want to make (knives, axes, tools, gates, sculpture, etc.). With these end goals in mind, your shop can be adjusted accordingly in size and tooling as it evolves. However, I believe that no matter your end goal, the start should be relatively the same for everyone getting started in this boundless craft. As a beginner, your objectives will be different than those of a seasoned smith, and it's important to let your shop reflect current goals. I would avoid over-planning and wait to build or obtain optimal equipment not necessary for your current skill level or situation. Oftentimes purchasing expensive equipment or building a large shop when you are only a beginner can be detrimental to long term learning due to the potential experiences and lessons lost from using hand tools.

For most of you beginning in blacksmithing, end goals may be undefined. This is expected, as your goals will almost definitely change as you begin putting hours under your belt at the forge.

You may find that knife making isn't really for you and that making hardware and tools is your passion (good thing you didn't start off with purchasing that $4,000 knife grinder).

By showing you how to be efficient, acquire skills, and build creativity, I hope that this book can encourage you to begin building a blacksmithing shop and let your creativity express itself.

Here is an example from my own life of the benefits derived from efficiency, a sharp learning curve, and creativity:

I mentioned in the preface about my success in the 2016 "Forged in Fire" competition. What I did not say was that it was in part due because I had spent six years (thousands of hours) in a very small (one-hundred-square-foot) space, forging with the help of duct-tape-handled tools on a dirt floor in subfreezing winter temperatures. Like Rocky Balboa when he trained to face his Russian opponent, I had learned more valuable and versatile methods and skills in my small shed by myself than any number of expensive, high-end tools could have taught me. I believe that the payoff of working in a minimalist shop—efficiency, rapid learning, and creativity—helped me meet the challenges that I faced that day in Brooklyn.

A well rounded and experienced craftsman understands how to perform a job in multiple ways with the tools provided. If you have a deep understanding of the craft and the courage to fail, then no challenge can stop you. This understanding is more important than any amount of equipment, and the goal of this book is to convince you of this truth.

Photos from Forged in Fire, courtesy of History Channel

Essential tools

This chapter is for those of you who are unsure of which tools are essential, which tools are not essential, and how to acquire truly needed tools at low cost or by making them yourself. There are very few tools essential to begin blacksmithing. In fact, I started with things lying around the house, and most of you can too. Why is this? The reason is that very little has changed over centuries of blacksmithing. A rudimentary shop, which many of you will be making for yourselves, might seem familiar to blacksmiths working in the 1700s. Like much else in blacksmithing, consider putting together your own shop as an exercise in ingenuity.

Four fundamental tools are needed to forge metal: an anvil, a hammer, tongs, and a fire pit or forge. Before describing each of these tools in turn, the question arises: should you make your own tools or buy them? The answer depends on your particular goals and on the progress you have already made in blacksmithing. As this book is aimed toward beginners, it is assumed that your time at the forge is going to earn less money for you than what you earn from other sources. Therefore, making your own tools frees up scarce money for other necessities. But even if that is not the case, when you first learn blacksmithing, making your own tools brings with it enormous benefits by accelerating your movement up the learning curve. My suggestion is making as many tools yourself as possible, which is both a cheaper and more satisfying option.

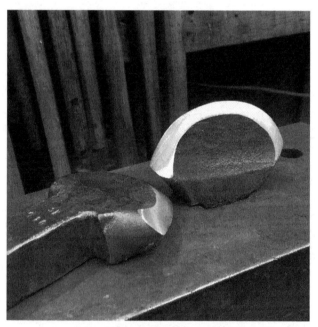

Hand-forged, hot-cut hardies

Here are three specific tools that you should consider making for yourself:

Hand Punches

This is a very easy tool project that you can start as a beginner. Making a round punch involves forging a simple round taper. Heat treating the striking end is optional and not required. Punches can be made with square ends to create square holes as well or used for center punches as pictured. Round punches will be used to create holes in your projects as an alternative to a drill.

Hand-forged center punch, round taper

Tongs

Once you have made your punch, you have at hand a tool that you have made that will help in making your next tool, a pair of tongs. Tongs are a fantastic project for a beginner, which is why I teach it in my basic blacksmithing class. In order to make tongs, a variety of techniques are brought into play: square taper, round taper, fullering, forging offsets using the "half-on, half-off" technique, punching, drifting, and making and assembling a rivet. In the making of a simple pair of tongs, you can learn an array of skills that will help you with other projects in the future. I highly recommend trying your hand at forging a pair of rudimentary tongs before you get too far down the rabbit hole. You can find tutorials online on how to do this with step-by-step instructions.

Variety of jaw types on hand forged tongs

Hand forged RR spike tongs

Hand Fullers

Fullers are tools designed to forge indentations in projects and are primarily used as tools to direct the movement of steel more accurately than a hand hammer can. Fullers can be made in different radiuses to your liking. These can be made similar to hand punches but with a flared and rounded end.

How many tools you decide to make for yourself will depend on how much you feel you are learning from the process and how soon you feel the need to actually sell projects from your shop. Making the tools yourself will help you in two ways: you'll learn the processes of forging them and the fundamental skills that forging these tools can teach you, as well as having the satisfaction of using tools that you have made. You'll find that there are many smaller tools and various specific tooling that you'll need in order to finish certain projects as you go along. Here are some other common tools that you'll need to acquire over time that you may decide to make for yourself: specialized tongs and hammers, an array of fullers, hardy tools and holdfasts, and punches and chisels.

As you start building up your tool collection, your skills will advance, and you'll be able to

Hand-forged bottom fuller

Hand-forged top fullers

take on more difficult tool projects with newfound confidence and with a growing array of tools to assist you. A more difficult project for a beginner would be forging a hardy tool or hammer. Hardy tools and hammers require using larger stock, which is difficult to work with using minimal tools and help; however, it can be done with the right tongs and a friend swinging a sledgehammer. Work your way up from the bottom, starting with simple punches and drifts and then tongs, and find your way from there. By building your tool selection by yourself, you will advance in skill quickly, whereas if you simply buy all of your easy-to-make tools, you can lose the experience this will provide. If an early project requires a too-hard-to-make tool, then the best option may be to find a new or

Hand-forged center punches

Hand forged 8lb sledge hammer

used tool online (see suggestions under online material and tool suppliers).

Once you become an intermediate-level blacksmith or professional, your time is worth far more than the price of a tool. Moreover, the additional skills generated from further tool making won't create such a profound impact as they would on a beginner. After two or three years of steady, constant practice under your belt, you will probably decide to purchase many tools that you already know how to make because your time is now more valuably spent on turning out product. Nevertheless, many master smiths continue to make advanced tools such as small anvils or beautifully forged leg vises.

A Brief Note on Types of Steel

Before discussing the four essential tools that you will use in your shop, a brief description of the various types of steel is in order. As a beginner, you should avoid forging and finishing steels that are outside of your skill parameters, as heat treating such steels at a starter level can ruin your projects and just waste your time in areas where you could be practicing on fundamentals. For starter projects use mild steel, which has a low carbon content (steel = iron + carbon, Fe+C) and may not be hardened by quenching. It will be safe to dunk in water and oil, and easy to drill through and forge. Mild steel is the least expensive alloy of steel available and is easily accessible from a welding shop, online source, or junkyard. Just make sure it is a mild steel! It will be great for anything except a blade or tool that is subject to deformation with use.

Mild Steel

This is a readily available structural steel that is not capable of being hardened by quenching. Its typical chemistry is *around* 97 percent iron, 0.18 percent carbon, 0.80 percent manganese, and a hint of phosphorous and sulfur added into the mix. It is easily machinable and workable cold or hot.

Hooks, practice pieces, gates, ornamental ironwork, and sculptures are made using mild steel. It's important that you understand how to use a simple steel before getting your head wrapped around heat treating correctly.

REBAR

Rebar is made in various grades for different construction projects. It is usually made of recycled steel but still has to meet specific maximum and minimum requirements such as tensile strength, corrosion resistance, and so forth. We aren't typically able to pinpoint exactly what alloy a piece of rebar found at a scrapyard is. However, rebar is consistently softer than medium- and high-carbon steels, making it easy to work and fairly forgiving for the beginner to work with. Its main advantage is the added toughness and flexibility it provides in a finished product without heat treating. This is what makes it great for tongs.

Rebar is a great source for a lower-carbon steel. Even though it is not actually mild steel, it is mild enough to be usable for beginner projects. It does not need to be heat treated and has a great spring to it when finished. I actually prefer to use rebar for my tongs due to its springiness. It's very inexpensive and can often be found at junkyards or in leftover pieces found free from a concrete supply business. Rebar is available in round sizes up to one and one-eighth of an inch typically. You can even get creative with incorporating the rebar texture into your artwork.

3/8th's rebar

High carbon steel

Using high carbon steels and tool steels mean heat treating is involved, and this is a subject for an entirely separate book. Tool steels and high carbon steels are also harder to forge when red hot. Stay away from them for now. Common mild steels are 1018 and A36. Stop by your local welding shop and see if they will cut a small amount of mild steel to last you a few months of practice. Now that you have a better idea of how to start, let's go over the essential tools needed at your shop.

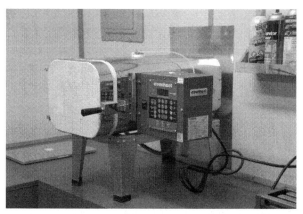

Professional heat treating oven for high carbon and tool steels

What you need

No blacksmith can work without a hammer and anvil, a forge, and a pair of tongs. Each of these four tools deserve further extensive discussion.

> **Liam's Tip:**
> **The best tool is often the one you have.**

Anvils

On the anvil, all of your work will be forged and created from raw pieces of steel. The anvil is the foundation and centerpiece of the shop, an ancient tool dating as far back as 6000 BC. The anvil has evolved in size, shape, and construction over thousands of years. The earliest of anvils were made of rock, bronze, and iron from meteorites. The anvil played such an important role in early technology and culture that in many civilizations it was worshiped as a symbol of strength and was even used in marriage rituals around the world. Many of us may picture the classic English or London pattern anvil, which was popularized in the 1800s after years of adaptation. This anvil is the most famous pattern and exemplifies the evolved geometry preferred by many.

London-pattern anvil

Early anvils were cast from nonferrous alloys, whereas many anvils made in the nineteenth and early twentieth centuries were forged from multiple smaller pieces of wrought iron, which were then forge welded together. After the wrought-iron base is constructed, another forge weld is used to attach a tool steel top plate, which is resistant to wear and increases the anvil's performance.

Rebound is paramount to the quality of an anvil, allowing the blacksmith to work longer without tiring. The mass, construction, and materials used in an anvil affect rebound. Rebound can be observed as the amount of bounce returned from a hammer blow—the more, the better. If you're anvil hunting, take a ball bearing or small hammer with you and gently drop it from twelve inches above the face of the anvil. If the ball bearing or hammer rebounds seven to twelve inches from the anvil, it has a desirable rebound. Rebound is not necessary on your first anvil, but it is something to look for when purchasing an anvil later on.

The geometry of the anvil helps with specific tasks. The main face of the anvil is used for the bulk of your work, including shaping, drawing material out, flattening, rounding, tapering, punching, and doing other general forge work.

Cast-iron "oil field" bridge anvil

The horn of the anvil is used for bending, shaping, and fullering operations.

Over the years, anvils developed two distinct holes (square and round) in the heel of the anvil. These are called the hardy hole and the pritchel hole. The square hardy hole makes possible a wide array of versatility in use of the anvil by allowing different tools to be added to the face of it, such as fullers, spring swages, hot cuts, or other specific tooling. The round pritchel hole is used less frequently and serves

Old Austrian "church-window" style anvil

primarily as an area for small drifting operations or in farrier operations. Alternatively, the pritchel hole has been used to hold other tools and jigs such as a holdfast.

The anvil shelf is a small area between the horn and main face and is used as a sacrificial area for cutting stock, punching, and other abusive tasks to take place. It's imperative not to perform these abusive tasks on the primary face of the anvil in order to prevent wear. The horn and main face should remain pristine on a quality anvil, and it takes practice with your hammer not to damage them. Lending an anvil to an inexperienced smith risks damage to this very valuable tool.

The weight distribution on an anvil is also key to its performance. If the heel is thinner rather than thicker, then heavier forging and hardy tool operations are not as suitable. Some anvils have more mass under the main face than others, and horn size will vary from anvil to anvil. Over time, you will develop an eye and a preference for specific anvil shapes and orientations. The German anvil provides an excellent example of extreme mass under the main face and is preferred by many blacksmiths. What if you cannot get your hands on one of these "real" anvils? Don't worry; you can start with an item around your house or visit a scrapyard and hunt for a thick, heavy piece of steel, preferably sixty-plus pounds. If you're using a smaller anvil, be sure to mount it securely to minimize play. The better the anvil is secured, the less power will be lost in your hammer strikes. Nevertheless, it is important to understand what is preferred in an anvil and what is not.

North German pattern anvil, photo from
Matchless Antiques - http://blacksmithbarn.com/

Hammers

Hammers work synergistically with the blacksmith's anvil, and different styles of hammers have different uses. Similar to the rebound of an anvil, a properly hardened hammer will also have rebound, increasing forging efficiency. A hammer's weight distribution also affects its performance similarly to the anvil. Most cross-peen hammers have an even amount of mass on either side of the hammer eye. Japanese-styled hammers and cutlers' hammers have the majority of their mass on one side, giving the hammer a very distinct heavy-forward feel. Different cultures have developed different types of hammers, and while they all serve the same basic

(Left to right) Rounding hammer, Swedish cross peen, French cross peen

purpose, they each work differently. The most well-known blacksmith hammer is the German cross peen. There are also French, Italian, Czech, English, and Swedish as well as other cross peen hammers.

A hammer that has gained increasing acceptance recently is the rounding hammer, popular among farriers. Rounding hammers are two sided: one with a flat face, the other rounded. The flat face is used for flattening and general forging, while the round face moves

Four-pound rounding hammer

Swedish cross peen

Hand-forged German cross peen with a Damascus steel face

material quickly and efficiently. By striking your material with a rounded face, your force is focused more directly rather than being spread out by the surface area of a flat die. In theory, one should begin forging with the round face to quickly draw out material and then flip the hammer around in order to flatten the work piece. The versatility and balance of these hammers have quickly shot them up to the top of the forging hammer world.

Ball peen hammers are common in every metal worker's shop; however, in the blacksmith shop, they have limited purpose in forging operations. The primary task that a ball peen hammer has in forging is to help in doming rivets on tongs or ornamental and structural ironwork with the

Hand-forged ball peen hammer

round ball peen end. A ball peen is often used in other shop work as a general utility hammer or in knife making to hammer small pins and dome work pieces.

Preferences and tastes in hammers develop over time, so don't get stuck on them at this point. Right now we need to focus on simply having something that we can hammer with in order to get started immediately. Any hammer will do in a pinch, even a framing hammer or small steel mallet.

Tongs

Tongs are one of four fundamental items needed to begin blacksmithing. Without them, you're limited to only being able to work on longer pieces of stock that can be held by hand. Tongs can be replaced by pliers or vise grips temporarily. Blacksmiths' tongs can be bought new online for around forty dollars, found at flea markets, or made by you as previously recommended.

Quality tongs should have a flex and springiness to them when gripped while holding the work piece securely with no chance of slipping. A hot piece of steel falling on your toes serves as a reminder to acquire a higher-quality pair of tongs. If you take the route of making your own tongs, I recommend using rebar as an inexpensive source for tong stock. Rebar is harder than mild steel and has a good amount of spring to it when made into tongs. If buying steel online, 1045 carbon steel, a medium-carbon, water-hardening steel, will produce a quality set of tongs. However, if you do use 1045 steel, do not heat treat them. They will retain a spring to them naturally.

There are numerous styles of tongs in use with some tongs made for one specific job. The two most common styles of tongs that the beginner should have are flat jaw tongs and wolf jaw tongs. Flat jaw tongs have the simplest jaw type in that the jaws are flat and clamp down on to other flat surfaces. These will be good if you plan to forge and grip flat stock on many different types of projects.

Wolf jaw tongs are versatile, featuring numerous holding positions for flat, round, or square stock. My first tool purchase was a pair of forty-dollar wolf jaw tongs (a big deal for me financially at the time). These allowed me to hold and work on many different projects without changing tongs, and I still use them in my shop today.

Forges

The fourth fundamental tool needed to start blacksmithing is the forge or heat source. Without the forge, steel cannot be heated enough to become red hot and malleable. It is worth noting that red-hot steel is similar in hardness to cold aluminum or copper, depending on the exact temperature and steel alloy being forged. A forge is simply a concentrated fire big enough to accommodate a piece of steel to be heated, with a forced air source added to increase the temperature of the fire. While there are numerous types of forges, we're going to focus on three primary types differentiated by what fuel they burn.

Coal forge at full blast

Charcoal and Wood-Burning Forges

Charcoal and wood-burning forges are among the most primitive and simple to build and use. When I first began, I heated steel using firewood and a hairdryer as an air source.

Wood will not burn as hot or as long as charcoal will. Charcoal is most commonly used in Japanese forges today, and good examples of these forges can be found on YouTube. I recommend using charcoal or wood as a starting heat source as it's easy and widely available.

If you are in a rural setting, a simple forge can be built using cinder blocks and a hair dryer at the base of the fire that blows air to the center. The more contained your fire is, the hotter it will become. In an urban environment, a simple forge can be built using charcoal briquettes in an old grill or on top of a piece of metal. The hair dryer is the go-to air source option for home blacksmithing enthusiasts and beginners as it's obtained easily and inexpensively. It can be positioned at the side of your forge and angled downward to the center of the fire. With the right amount of air, your fire will become hot enough to melt steel, so be careful. If you are using too much air, it will cause the opposite effect, so playing around with your air source is important to obtaining the correct heat.

COAL-BURNING FORGES

Coal forges are the most traditional of all blacksmithing forges and are used by both beginners and master blacksmiths. I have nearly six years of experience forging with coal. The coal forge is very similar to the charcoal or wood-burning forge in its construction.

Coal forge burning green coal

Coal needs an air source, and just like wood, the position of the air source is often forced into the side of the fuel or underneath the fire pot itself. Designing and fabricating a forge with a bottom blast design is more time consuming and difficult for those who want to get started with minimal cost and time. In addition, it's important to understand how coal works and what's happening over the course of its burning. When you buy coal, it will come as green coal, which is denser and darker than its later stage, called coke. Green coal is full of impurities, and once these impurities and tar bubble and burn off in the form of yellow or white smoke, the coal transforms into coke.

When the transformation of coal to coke takes place, the impurities that are not burned off in smoke gather in the bottom of the forge's air blast and form what's called a clinker. A clinker is a conglomerate of silica, ash, and other impurities from coal. Untended, the clinker will clog your air source and add impurities to your work. You must be diligent in removing the clinker soon after it has formed to maintain an efficient fire.

> **Liam's tip:**
> A lesser but steadier air flow through your forge's air gate is advantageous over a temporary strong air flow that is only open while your work piece is in the forge.

Coke is desired in a forge, and the smith will constantly be monitoring and adjusting the fire to transform coal into coke. Coke is porous and burns hotter and cleaner than coal, and it does not produce smoke or excessive gasses after the coal to coke transformation is complete. It is neither usual nor recommended to forge steel in a green coal fire. Doing so would allow tar and pollutants to adhere to the steel, causing problems with forge welding and with reaching desired temperatures for forging. Managing a coal forge is a skill in and of itself and should be taken into account before deciding to forge with coal.

It is worth noting that coal produces toxic byproducts when burned, including but not limited to selenium, chromium, mercury, cadmium, arsenic, and lead. Scared yet? This alone is a deterrent for many smiths; however, this doesn't prevent a large number of blacksmiths from using this heating source. At around six cents a pound (depending on location), coal can be the least expensive fuel option for the hobbyist. Although widespread among shops around the world of old, its use has been diminishing as smiths switch to propane and other heat sources. While the practice of burning coal may allow us a glimpse of the past, it isn't the fuel source for everyone.

Pictured on the next page is how a simple charcoal or coal forge is constructed. A basic coal or charcoal burning forge will consist of a table, fire pot, a tuyere (see nearby diagram), a blower, and an ash dump. The fire pot is typically four to eight inches in depth with a width and length of around eight to twelve inches. The fire pot should contain burning coals and not have areas that aren't getting hot. The rest of your forge's table will hold your unburned fuel reservoir. If the fire pot is too deep, it will take too long to heat up your entire fire, and you'll end up burning more fuel than necessary. It may take some trial and error to determine the right size fire pot for you. As a beginner, I would stay on the smaller side in order to prevent excessive fuel burn and time lost in managing a large fire. A small fire is all that is needed for basic projects.

If you're building your own fire pot, use a minimum of ¼-inch-thick plate steel, although 3/8-inch thick is optimum since heat and

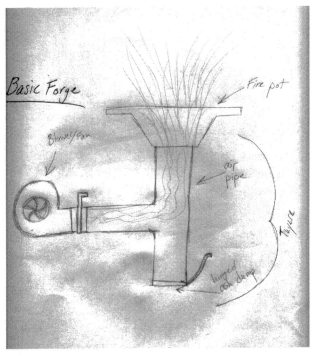

Basic forge construction

impurities from coal will corrode the steel over time and eventually require that it be replaced. And no one wants to do that. Four to six evenly spaced air holes of 3/8- to 5/8-inch diameter drilled in the bottom of the fire pot suffice to distribute airflow properly. Don't drill excessive air holes as you can lose too many coals through the bottom of the fire pot. The table on a forge is not necessary, but it is convenient for tool placement and fuel storage. Many forges

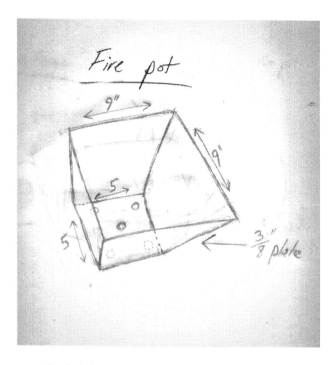

use firebrick or clay for the table and lining of the forge, but steel alone works as well.

The tuyere is the area underneath the fire pot that channels air into the fire pot. A tuyere needs to be large enough in diameter to deliver adequate airflow and distribute the air evenly across the pot's air holes. The blower on the forge can be a cheap hair dryer or better yet a squirrel cage blower, many of which can be purchased for under one hundred dollars. I recommend adding an air gate in front of the blower to allow greater control of your airflow as

Fire pot on my own coal forge

often the blower is too strong at full strength, and can easily melt your steel when not paying attention. An aluminum air gate can be bought online for around fifteen dollars.

If you want to go the no-electricity route, you can find older hand crank blowers online for $100–$200, depending on the condition. These are great for festivals or to provide a historic feel at home. One of my earliest forges used a turn-of-the-century Champion brand hand crank blower. I used this blower for a couple years, savoring its great old-time feel. However, my work production increased once I tried an electric blower, and I never went back.

The ash dump on the forge is situated at the bottom of the T-shaped pipe and collects particles that fall through the air holes in the fire pot. Every now and then, open the ash dump to maintain a constant airflow in the pipe. A simple cap with a hinge and counterweight welded on the ash dump works.

Early 1900's Champion hand crank blower

Propane-Burning Forges

Propane, a third heating source, has gained tremendous popularity within the blacksmithing community in recent years. For the beginner, propane is the most expensive in terms of setup and fuel cost. In the United States in 2016, the average cost per gallon of propane was $2.50. Obviously, this is far more expensive than six cents a pound for coal, and there are additional costs from building or purchasing a propane forge. Beginners could spend approximately fifteen dollars more on propane than on coal during each afternoon session.

Let's review the numerous positive aspects of burning propane. It is clean, easy to use, and fast. Propane, unlike coal, emits no foul odor,

Double-burner propane forge at full blast

Ignition of a propane forge

nor are there life-threatening side effects in its byproducts in a ventilated area. If you are asthmatic, I highly recommend choosing propane as your heat source. I've seen a blacksmith with asthma at a coal forge wearing a respirator, and it doesn't look like fun.

Propane is far easier to work with than charcoal and especially coal. It requires very little fire maintenance, allowing the beginner to focus on hammering steel and not building a fire. Maintenance with propane would include adjusting the regulator's pressure according to the work at hand, refilling the tanks regularly, and fixing the lining in the forge every year or so.

Propane forges heat up fast and allows you to begin work shortly after igniting your forge, whereas there can be twenty minutes of prep work alone in a coal forge before work can

Billet of Damascus steel heating in a Chile forge

begin. Propane forges can be left alone while heating more safely than a coal or charcoal forge can, and when finished with a propane forge, all that needs to be done is to shut off the propane valves. By contrast, after using a coal or charcoal forge, the fire pot needs to be cleaned and coals put out safely. All of these attributes make propane forges highly convenient and almost required in a residential area or garage-type setting. A home-built propane forge with burners can cost $100 for a quick, crudely built forge capable of heating small projects and up to $500 for a well-thought-out and well-designed forge with decent burners. A manufactured forge will cost approximately $400 for a hobbyist-level brand and up to $1,500 for a professional forge that will withstand the rigors of production work.

For the experienced smith who produces forged work in high quantity, propane forges are far cheaper than coal forges since the time they save the professional outweighs their higher fuel cost. I made the switch from coal to propane in early 2016, and my production increased dramatically.

For example, if I'm limited to forging two axes at a time in a coal forge, and it takes the same amount of time as forging ten axes at a time in a propane forge (due to the time consuming maintenance of coal), then the eventual potential gross sales from ten finished axes, at $250 an axe, is $2,000 higher in finished axe sales in the same amount of time as forging in coal. If we use 2.5 hours as a set time to forge two axes in coal, that equates to $200 of finished axes an hour in the coal forge with approximately $0.90 in coal at an assumed rate of fifteen pounds of coal in 2.5 hours. With propane, forging ten axes in the same 2.5 hours becomes $1,000 of axes an hour with $19 in propane, assuming we burn around 7.5 gallons. Propane only becomes less expensive if you are producing in high quantity. As this book is aimed toward very low initial setup costs, I don't recommend propane for beginners (except when absolutely necessary).

Fuel Source Comparison Chart

Fuel	Pro	Con
Propane	-Clean burning -Easy to use -Good for production work -No chimney needed	-Expensive fuel -More complex to build.
Coal	-Inexpensive fuel -Historic feel -Easy to build -Builds character	-Dirty -Produces toxic byproduct -Requires more maintenance than propane -Need exhaust hood
Wood or charcoal	-Inexpensive fuel -Easy to build -Burns cleaner than coal, but not as clean as propane	-Consumes large amount of fuel -Produces extreme radiant heat -Requires more maintenance than propane -Need exhaust hood

Luxury Tools

We have discussed the four essential and fundamental tools needed to begin forging: hammer, anvil, tongs, and the forge. Since the theme of this book centers on starting blacksmithing at a low cost, the following tools are deemed luxuries better obtained at a later date if you do not already have them. How soon they should be acquired depends on how far you have moved along your personal learning curve, how soon productivity (volume of output) begins to matter, and your financial situation. In general, patience is counseled as well as avoidance of the "buying skills" temptation. There are some tools that will be considered more of a luxury than others, and this comes down to the type of projects you're working on and in what quantity you will be producing them.

Very few to none of the luxury tools are 100 percent necessary as the processes they perform can be carried out with simple hand tools but at a slower and more difficult pace.

For example, if you are making knives with hidden tang guards that require a slot, then there are multiple ways to make the slot in the guard. This can be done by punching and drifting the guard material while hot for a crude fit. It can be done by using a hand drill to create pilot holes and then filing the inside out by hand. It can be done with an end mill in a drill press, and it can be done by using a hobbyist- or professional-grade milling machine. All methods work to an extent, the last being the most expensive but most effective on a larger scale. The first methods can be achieved with our essential tools and with tools that are already lying around your house.

Vises

Vises provide the blacksmith with a third hand. They are needed for projects that require a twist in them. The two types of vises used by blacksmiths are the bench vise and the post leg vise. Both serve the same basic purpose, but they differ widely in price and availability.

The bench vise is the most common type of vise on the market. Wilton is a well-recognized brand that can be bought new or restored to working order from junked or discarded older models. My current bench vise is a 1950s Wilton bullet vise, and I couldn't ask for anything more. Bullet vises are a type of bench

Post leg vise assisting in a twisting operation

Restored Wilton bullet vise

vise with an enclosed thread that allows for a wider opening and greater protection of the threads. Such vises can be found online or at yard sales at prices ranging anywhere from $10 for an old beater to $250 for a legacy tool that just needs a little cleanup. New vises, on the other hand, can cost thousands of dollars, depending on the model.

When looking for a vise, keep in mind the intended use. The most important factor is the size of the projects that you intend to engage with since vises come with different jaw sizes that obviously impose limits on project size. A four-inch jaw is typical on a bench vise. *Use of a bench vise for hot work is not recommended.*

Bullet vise with enclosed threads in the "bullet"

Post leg vises are the vises usually found in the blacksmith's shop. They stand around 3.5 feet tall and typically weigh between 70 and 100 pounds. The distinct leg of this vise serves both as a stability point, when mounted to the floor, and as a shock absorber. Post leg vises are designed to take a beating from a blacksmith's hammer, whereas a bench vise is not. I use my

Five inch post leg vise

post leg vise frequently to clamp something and wail on it to fix a bend or to cause a bend in heavy stock. Doing this causes the entire bench to shake, but the vise stays true. These vises are extremely handy in a forge shop and can be counted as one of the more necessary of the luxury items discussed here.

New post leg vices are scarce and expensive. However, post leg vices are among many legacy tools that have been made in such a durable form that they are capable of functioning for another generation or two. Post leg vises can be found most easily online or at blacksmith shows and conferences. A working post leg vise in the four- to six-inch jaw range will command a price around $300 depending on your local market. Once you get the vise into your shop, all that's to be done is to secure it to a bench or sturdy post and run the leg into the floor for shock distribution.

GRINDERS

Grinders replace hand filing, thereby greatly expediting the finishing process of pieces such as knives and other bladed tools. Depending on the type of blacksmithing work you decide to pursue, a grinder may be more or less needed. For many artist blacksmiths, a hand file or simply nothing at all is required as the piece is forged to the finish. On the opposite end of the spectrum, a knife maker needs a grinder to properly clean and shape the finished product even after forging the blade to shape.

Hundreds of different types and brands of grinders, both pneumatic and electric, are available in the marketplace. The three primary grinder types in the blacksmith's shop are the bench grinder, belt grinder, and angle grinder.

Electric and pneumatic angle grinders are the most common type of grinder in the metalworker's shop. These can be bought online or in a local hardware store for around seventy dollars. The angle grinder comes in different sizes, but the most typical size fits a 4.5-inch abrasive disc. The abrasive options are pretty widespread but more aimed toward heavier stock removal with a lack of finesse. These grinders are a fantastic tool that typically get used on a daily basis, from heavy stock removal to cutting metal in half with a cut-off disc. Angle grinders will work best for rough forgings or work done by tool makers, sculptors, or blacksmiths creating structural works of art.

Using an angle grinder on "Forged in Fire," photo courtesy of the History Channel

For bladesmiths, the angle grinder will have limited use.

While bench grinders are smaller and less versatile than belt grinders, they are also less expensive and can serve all the smith's basic needs. Bench grinders are fitted with round stone wheels of varying grits that attach to an arbor on the machine. They are great for rough stock removal in a simple shop. Typical cost for a bench grinder varies between $70 for a hardware store special and $200 for a top-quality name-brand tool.

Belt grinders are the preferred choice for fabricators and knife makers working today. These grinders provide the highest versatility in grits and operations. Belt grinders are equipped with different belt lengths and widths, but they are common in a 2 × 72 size (2 inches wide × 72 inches long). Belt grinders use an abrasive belt that is spun on a drive wheel and runs along different contact wheels or platens to deliver the actual grinding operation. Extensive tooling and belt options make this grinder an excellent choice for any type of finishing and grinding on wood or metal. The cost of a 2 × 72 grinder for knife makers and other fabricators ranges dramatically depending on the brand and quality. A $500 belt grinder, like the Grizzly grinder, can be all you need for small fabrication or as a hobby-level knife maker. It certainly won't perform like a Wilmont or Wuertz per se, but it can get the job done. Belt grinders built from high-end components with well-thought-out designs can cost around $4,000, but this isn't necessary or recommended for the beginner. Common brands used by knife makers include grinders by Grizzly, Bader, Burr King, KMG (by Beaumont Metal Works), Wuertz, and Wilmont. Other brands are also available, but the beginning smith should certainly evaluate one or more grinders from this list and then use them as points of comparison when looking at other brands.

Wilmont Triple Arm Grinder

KMG grinder by Beaumont Metal Works

Disc grinders are tools that cater to a far smaller group of metalworkers and don't provide a substantial payoff for the price of the machine unless you're using it frequently on knives. The disc grinder cannot perform heavy stock removal and is limited in abrasive options. In a general blacksmith shop setting, you will not often see a disc grinder, and it's a tool that we would consider more of a luxury than the other luxury items being discussed. It certainly has no use in making axes, tools, gates and furniture, sculptures, or knickknacks. The disc grinder really pays off when grinding and finishing flat knife blades or other flat components in knife making. Without a doubt it makes a knife maker's life easier, but it's not worth the investment unless you're halfway down the rabbit hole in a knife-making career.

Typical disc grinder size is nine inches in diameter, which allows the use of standard sheet-sized sandpaper to be applied to the disc using spray adhesive. Using the correct spray adhesive is key so the sandpaper can be removed easily after it is worn. I use either 3M Feathering Disc Adhesive Type 11 or a spray made by Quality Aerosol Q6000. Do not use the store-bought 3M Super 77 spray adhesive; this is not meant for our intended application on a disc grinder. Once the metal disc has been applied with adhesive, it will be good for five to ten sheets of sandpaper. Once it's time to change the adhesive, it's also helpful to have a spray cleaner that can easily remove it. I use 3M General Purpose Adhesive Cleaner. This is nasty stuff, so wear gloves. Alternatively, you can buy PSA (pressure sensitive adhesive) discs, which will stick on to the disc without spray adhesive, but these are expensive. I currently use a KMG nine-inch disc grinder with a VFD (variable frequency drive) from Beaumont Metal Works. Typical cost for a high-end disc grinder is around $1,200.

Nine-inch disc with variable speed and reverse settings

Buffers

Buffers are less common in a general blacksmith shop as compared with the shops of knife makers or jewelers. Buffers serve a very limited purpose: they make things shiny, to a mirror finish in most cases. In my shop, the buffer is only used to polish small areas on knives or axes. Buffers also can be used to remove a burr from the cutting edge of a blade.

Buffers are most common in six-inch and eight-inch wheel sizes and can be fitted with different types of buffing wheels such as sewn muslin or even Scotchbrite. After wheel selection, the buffing wheel is loaded with a specific buffing compound to achieve the desired finish. Some compounds produce a perfect mirror finish on steel; other compounds produce specialized finishes for nonferrous metals or wood. Certain buffing compounds are impregnated with grit so as to cut metal in a manner similar to a grinder. Buffing procedures offer a similar progression of grits as is offered by sandpaper. One starts with a low or coarse grit compound and ends with a grit that produces a mirror finish.

Baldor buffer with 8 inch buffing wheels

Loading pink compound on a buffing wheel

> **Liam's tip:**
> **Buffers can be a very versatile finishing tool. Research and learn which compounds do what on different wheels. This can replace a lot of grinding and hand work.**

Dedicated buffers are definitely a luxury item. As an alternative to a dedicated buffer, a bench grinder can be fitted with a buffing wheel to serve as dual-purpose machine. Baldor makes a great buffer that's still made in the United States. A buffer suitable for knife making costs around $500 for a top-of-the-line model. It is worth noting that buffers are a very dangerous machine if you are using them to polish knife blades. The buffer's fabric wheel can easily catch the knife on a corner or sharp edge and take it out of your hands, potentially inflicting serious injury or death. *It is recommended that you fabricate a guard at the back of the wheel in order to prevent knives or other objects from coming back around and hitting you.*

Swage Blocks

These interesting tools are used as forming and punching apparatuses. Similar to anvils in weight, these blocks have differently sized and shaped holes going through the center. The blocks also have forms on the sides that are used for bending metal into different curves to shape tools and ornamental projects. There are two types of swage blocks, one type that has more holes through the center, and a second type that offers different dished-out shapes for curving objects. The swage blocks with holes through the center are ideal for punching and drifting hammers and axes. I use a 120-pound swage block with different round, square, and rectangular slots through the center in order to drift large axes. Swage blocks are typically soft

Swage block on end to make use of forming dies

and made from cast iron or a soft-cast steel. Not intended to serve as an anvil, swage blocks should be used for bending metal of differing shapes and contours or for punching through using the open areas. Swage blocks, currently fetching close to seven dollars per pound, are often more expensive than anvils. If you find one at a decent price and in good condition, snatch it.

Swage block on a wooden stand

Swage blocks are neither a necessary tool in the beginner's shop or even in some advanced shops. But they certainly have a rightful place in the hammer or axe maker's shop.

In producing small axes, I have virtually eliminated my use of the swage block. Instead, I use a small square tube fixed two feet from my press for light drifting operations that don't require being hit with a sledgehammer. This simple square tube located very close to the press speeds up my axe-forging process and makes it more efficient. I do still use the swage block (approximately nine feet away from the press) for steps that require a drift to be hammered heavily with a sledgehammer. Most forms and bending also can be done over a hardwood log. Exercising a bit of creativity will allow you to delay getting a swage block.

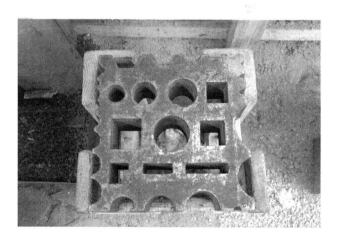

Drill Press

Drill presses greatly assist in the making of knives. However, punching and drifting techniques adequately serve the needs of ornamental blacksmiths' or beginners' holes. Through use of punching and drifting, the smith is able to fashion clean holes in ornamental sculptures, hooks, and the like. Because making steel knives requires a more precise method of creating holes, the drill press becomes necessary.

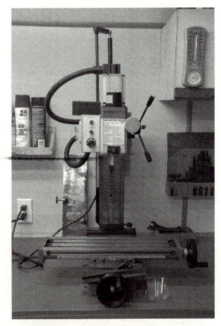

Bench top drill/mill combo tool

In a price range from $200 to $1,000, drill presses are not terribly expensive considering their payoff. A starter bench-top drill press for $200 can be picked up at your local hardware store and plugged into a regular 110v outlet. The drill press can also be adapted for shaping objects by carefully clamping them in the chuck and shaping them with sandpaper or other tools (similar to a lathe). Larger drill presses are necessary for drilling large diameter holes but not for the beginner.

POWER HAMMERS AND FORGING PRESSES

Power hammers and forging presses become indispensable at the point that your projects have become too large to forge by hand or if you are aiming for high-quantity production. Unnecessary for beginners, power hammers and presses are priced in the market starting around $4,000, a number well exceeding the total cost of a start-up shop.

What's the difference between power hammers and forging presses? The power hammer, in ram sizes usually starting at twenty-five pounds and going up, simulates the hammer strike of a blacksmith, whereas a press impacts the steel at low velocity. The power hammer is fast and best used for thinner stock or for drawing out long materials with less heat transfer from the work piece into the hammer die. The power hammer does not act as a heat sink as the press does. However, it is more difficult but not impossible to create specialized tooling for the power hammer. Another advantage of the power hammer over the forging press is that it comes in a wider range of weights and brands.

Air-powered, mechanical, and even water or steam-powered power hammers are available under brand names such as Little Giant, Nazel, Chambersburg, Sahinler, Say Mak, Bradley, and Anyang, among others. Earlier power hammers were powered with a water wheel. Self-contained air hammers are common today and provide the best control over the ram, affording extreme accuracy. Nazel self-contained hammers are popular and highly desired by many blacksmiths because they offer control, high quality, and an appropriate size for heavy work. Unfortunately, the Nazel is no longer made, and finding and restoring one can be expensive. The largest Nazel hammers virtually require that a shop be built around them; they are monstrous machines designed for factory production.

At the opposite extreme from Nazels, DIY power hammers are also available, such as the commonly known tire hammer. This tool can be found online and built by the smith in his or her own shop. Although tire hammers are not as highly powerful or controllable as manufactured hammers, they do allow quicker work than that done by hand hammer. Power hammers, boasting a long history in metal working, are the

Anyang 165 power hammer, photo courtesy of http://www.anyangusa.net/

most common machines used in forging in today's blacksmith's shop.

Hydraulic forging presses deliver far more power, pound for pound, than a power hammer of equivalent size. For example, a fifteen-hundred-pound (total machine weight) forging press can work steel of a size much larger than a fifteen-hundred-pound power hammer. Although hydraulic forging presses are less

Student forging on an Anyang 88 power hammer

common than power hammers (they were only introduced into the blacksmith's shop around 120 years ago), they are less expensive for the force they deliver. Hydraulic forging presses also take up a smaller shop footprint and can be used in a shop as small as one hundred square feet. Forging presses are usually more job specific than power hammers and excel at specialized tooling operations. This makes them a great machine for production work that requires specific tooling to create a product in a repeatable and consistent manner. Press dies are also much easier to change in and out of a hydraulic forging press than a power hammer.

Common tonnage on a hydraulic forging press outside of an industrial setting is fifteen, twenty-five, and fifty tons of force. A fifty-ton hydraulic forging press costs around $7,000 new and takes up no more room than a large band saw. Despite its small size, it can deliver as much force as a power hammer with a several-hundred-pound ram. I currently use a fifty-ton press and have not been limited by any size of steel.

The current limit on the size of my projects derives from the size of my forge, not from the size of my forging press. Presses also work well with stock over an inch thick, and they almost work better if the stock is thicker. When I was ready to buy one of these tools and had to choose between the power hammer and the

McNabb fifty-ton forging press

forging press, I ultimately chose the press because of its smaller size, delivery of immense force for it's relative size, and greater versatility when used with specialized dies. The forging press allows me to produce axes repeatedly and on a larger scale than I can with a hand hammer and with no loss in quality.

The forging press is also well suited for punching and drifting eyes in axes and hammers. If I were an artist blacksmith forging long tapers, I'd opt for the power hammer. Ideally, after several years, you'll have both of these machines in the shop. The downside of a hydraulic press is the speed of the ram and heat that is lost while using it. Again, the thicker the stock, the better on the press, as it doesn't lose heat quickly and works well when fifty tons of force are applied. I'm unable to move stock under one-quarter inch easily because there is little velocity on the press, and the heat is lost quickly into the thick dies. Luckily, the majority of my work is forged from large blocks of steel, and my press excels at forging hammers, axes, and other such tools.

I'm currently using a press made by Tommy McNabb (http://carolinaknives.com/products). A smaller press (sixteen to twenty-five tons) is available from Coal Iron Works. As of this writing, there are very promising things coming from Anyang for hydraulic forging presses. Finally, there is an option of building your own hydraulic press or power hammer. However, unless you're a skilled welder and fabricator, it's likely you will end up with an inferior piece of equipment that ultimately will cost more money in the end. I don't think I've yet seen a high-quality homemade press or hammer. Homemade tools seem to work OK for a little while and then inevitably become obsolete or broken after continual use. The time spent researching and building these machines, in my opinion, can be a waste of time. At the point you're at the skill level to rightfully own a power hammer or forging press, your time should be highly valued enough to justify working with a nice, new machine or well built legacy tool rather than spending time building a homemade "fool tool." However, there are always exceptions to every rule.

To summarize this last point in another way, at the very beginning, as you start up the learning curve, making simple tools yourself is both a way to learn and to save money. Later, and in fact at almost any stage, refurbishing well-made legacy tools can be both personally satisfying and money saving. Finally, with a well-developed skill set and the prospect of earning income from your work, diverting the additional time required to make sophisticated tools is likely to be expensive, unproductive, and frustrating.

Budget Shop Formulas

Let's put together three basic shops that can be sufficient for a month, a year, or the entirety of your blacksmithing endeavors. A $50 setup may work for one person, while a $300 setup may be *your* preferred starting point. A walled or even roof-only structure is not required for a beginner shop; however, it is recommended that a roof-only structure is at least used with a propane forge. Any simple lean-to or shed-type structure will suffice. Here are a few different starting points that can be applied as is or in different combinations.

SHOP 1

Approximate startup time - *one day*
Approximate startup cost - *zero dollars*
(Preferable for those who want a taste of forging with lowest initial investment)

Tools required	Source	Possible item
Hammer	Household item	Mallet, claw hammer, small sledge hammer
Anvil	Household item	Trailer hitch, farm implement, sledge hammer head, dumbbell
Tongs	Household item	Vise grips, pliers, channel locks
Fuel	Household item	Wood or charcoal around your house
Forge	Household item	Dugout pit, cinder block/brick construction, old grill, frying pan
Air source	Household item	Blow dryer

SHOP 2

Approximate startup time - *one week*
Approximate startup cost - *$270 to $400*

Tools required	Source	Approximate Price
Hammer	Local hardware store	$20
Anvil	Heavy steel object from local scrapyard	$10-100
Tongs	Online providers	$40
Fuel	Online and local providers	Lump charcoal (50lbs) $40 Green coal (50lbs) $3
Forge	Built by local welding shop	$200
Air source	Household item	**Blow Dryer**

SHOP 3

Approximate startup time - *one month*
Approximate startup cost - *$1150 to $1950*

Tools required	Source	Approximate Price
Hammer	Online providers	$75-200
150lb Anvil	Online from E-bay, Craigs list, or found locally at estate sales	$450
Three piece tong assortment	Online providers	$100
Propane fuel	100LB tank from local hardware store	$100 for tank $50 for fuel
Propane forge	Online providers	$350-1000

Safety

Understanding how to safely engage in blacksmithing is an important aspect of starting out in the craft and setting up a new shop. The risks associated with blacksmithing are many, ranging from what you might breathe in (metal fume fever), to what you might touch or what touches you (burns, abrasions), to how you handle your own bodily movements (repetitive stress injuries), to what you do to your hearing. Using personal protective equipment (PPE) is essential.

One slip of the tongs and you can be burned by near-molten steel; one stray spark off a grinder (or a wire spun off of a wire wheel) can cause you to lose or damage your eyesight; prolonged work without ear protection will cost you the ability to have normal conversations with family and friends without the use of a hearing aid. Traditionally, not wearing PPE was thought to be manly (or at least cool), but most modern blacksmiths have sensibly embraced protective gear as the wiser alternative to "macho" posturing.

Two friends of mine illustrate starkly diverging approaches to safety: Bob puts on safety glasses when he walks out the door in the morning and literally doesn't take them off until he goes to bed. Paul doesn't wear safety glasses because he finds them annoying. Bob and Paul are full-time bladesmiths at the top of their field. Not using some form of PPE while blacksmithing is simply a gamble with very bad odds; in this gamble, the "winner" gains nothing other than the chance to keep the health and well-being that he or she already had to begin with, while the "loser" forfeits sight, hearing, or even the ability to take a breath without agonizing difficulty. If we were sitting down calmly and were asked to think about this tradeoff, most of us would require a gun pointed at our heads before agreeing to the high-risk approach. Sadly, mistaken craft traditions (including myths), peer pressure, and misplaced displays of "machismo" have led even some experienced smiths to ignore proper use of PPE. The discussion that follows assumes that you will not be among this group.

There are four primary forms of PPE used in blacksmithing: safety glasses, hearing protection, gloves, and respirators. Workshop lighting and dust collection should be mentioned as well. Each of these factors will now be separately discussed, but it should be understood that they are woven together to form a crucial safety net that will allow you to healthfully participate in the blacksmithing craft. If there is one additional overarching piece of advice, it is this: "Habit," as William James observed, "is twice character." Bob does not even notice that he dons his safety glasses each morning; on the contrary, were he *not* to do so, he would immediately sense that something was wrong. As with Bob's morning ritual, each aspect of PPE has to be woven into your habitual routines even if it feels strange or unwieldy at first. Daily teeth flossing or buckling a seatbelt may also have felt unwieldy at first, yet most flossers or drivers notice these practices only if they are absent.

SAFETY GLASSES

Safety glasses are of such importance that they should be seen as a requirement before working near a forge or grinder. In multiple instances I have avoided potentially serious damage to my own eyesight only because I had been wearing safety glasses. Unfortunately, even *with* safety glasses your eyes remain at risk for damage. Over only eight years, I've had multiple pieces of metal pulled out of an eye, even while wearing glasses. I hate to think what would have happened if I hadn't been wearing them.

Safety glasses don't have to be fancy or expensive. I actually prefer the inexpensive kind (about three dollars from Amazon). In the past, I've used twenty-five-dollar safety glasses, but I find that they work no differently than the three-dollar kind. The idea is to have *some* form of glasses on when working, even if it means sunglasses or prescription glasses. Aside from clear safety glasses, you can also purchase specialized glasses from a welding supply store or online provider which are specially made for forge welding. Very few people use such glasses, but if you weld in your forge for hours every day, these may help prevent slight vision loss. For the occasional welder, these glasses are not essential.

HEARING PROTECTION

After the predominant need to protect your eyesight, protecting your hearing comes in second. There are many loud noises, some exceeding 100DB (decibels) in the shop. Regular ambient noise registers 60DB, just for comparison. Once you attack more difficult projects and obtain specialized power tools, the need for hearing protection increases. I would venture that relatively fewer people employ hearing protection than employ vision protection. This may be simply because most people value their eyes more than their long-term hearing, but I think a more subtle factor is at work. Vision damage or loss often occurs in a single, dramatic moment; hearing loss, on the other hand, is gradual, accumulating over months and years of exposure. It is easy to promise yourself that you'll get hearing protection "soon," but if you wait until symptoms appear—"Whaddya say?"—you have already waited too long. Like with osteoarthritis and other wear-and-tear damage to the body, hearing that is lost cannot be "cured," only mitigated by use of hearing aids. For me, the cost/benefit tradeoff for wearing hearing protection is an absolute no brainer. When I am twenty-five and have the chance at a hot date, I'm not planning to accessorize my look with a pair of hearing aids.

3M 105 earmuffs

Two main types of hearing protection are available: ear *muffs* and ear *plugs*. Ear plugs come in a disposable or reusable form. I think the advantages of plugs versus muffs are pretty evenly split, although I do prefer muffs. Muffs are more expensive, but they also last longer. After a few hours, muffs do tend to get uncomfortable. If you do decide on muffs, plan to buy a pair of more expensive, cushioned ones. A good pair (rated to protect over 100DB) is available for around fifty dollars. Remember, a somewhat pricier pair that you actually wear will provide more protection than the cheap pair that lies on the shelf because you do not find them to be comfortable.

Gloves

Gloves, as compared with ear protection, fall below the must-use threshold. Although nonessential, they do have their uses. I only wear a glove on my left hand when forging as my right hand is tied up using a hammer or other tools. Do not hammer with a glove on; this impairs your grip and limits dexterity. Ironically, using a glove as PPE while hammering actually makes hammering more dangerous. However, your nondominant tong hand can benefit from a glove since it is this hand that is more exposed to the risks of scale or slag. A glove helps prevent burns from loose scale and allows you to quickly pick up tools that may otherwise be too hot to handle.

I also use gloves when rough grinding to prevent burns and abrasions from course belts. Without protection, a twenty-four-grit ceramic belt can quickly chew down to your bone in a fraction of a second. The knuckles on my thumbs and index fingers are littered with scar tissue from bearing into a grinder without wearing gloves in the past. However, now whenever I rough grind an axe, I wear some form of protection for my fingers. There is no need for a special type of glove for grinding, just some layer of protection between your hands and the ever-so-fast-moving ceramic belt. The key to wearing gloves while grinding is tightness: tightly fitting gloves do not reduce dexterity as much as loose gloves do. Loose gloves pose a danger when using a grinder since they can get caught on moving belts. I still avoid gloves when I'm final grinding knives or working with delicate wood. I only use gloves when trying to "hog" off material as fast as possible.

My early opposition to wearing gloves while grinding evaporated after I had scraped my knuckles to bloody bones, and in the process losing some sensation in the nerves. I don't entirely regret it though. I take joy in learning from my mistakes and take pride in the numb scars on my knuckles as I'm now able to look back at what had happened as a reminder to never do it again. Even after wearing gloves at the grinder, I still slip and knock my fingers into the belt every now and then, but the glove is just enough to prevent damage to my skin. These little accidents ruin the gloves, but they're more replaceable than hands. As mentioned, if you are using gloves at the grinder, do not use baggy gloves, and be aware of all areas that your fingers are near. If your fingers are near a contact wheel or pinch point while gloved, you do run the risk of being sucked into the grinder. At the time of this writing, I'm currently wearing cut-resistant gloves found on amazon.com. These are inexpensive, abrasion resistant, fast drying, and tight fitting.

Leather welding gloves

In searching for gloves for heat protection, there are a few types of glove materials and other options in the marketplace. Leather gloves are cheap and easy to find locally. Andreas, my assistant, is a fan of leather gloves, and they seem to work well for him. These allow him to pick up hot punches and drifts as the job requires without burning himself. Leather gloves tend to shrink and harden over time; the rate at which this happens is increased by picking up hot things (that shrink your gloves). Since leather gloves are comparatively inexpensive, it is not too inconvenient to replace them periodically. Another potential downside of a leather glove is the loss of dexterity as leather welding gloves typically have a loose fit.

Kevlar gloves are a more expensive alternative to leather and can usually only be bought online, depending on where you live. Kevlar gloves range in price from $25 to $200 a pair and come with different added materials, including cotton. Kevlar gloves are rated and priced according to their ability to protect against various temperatures. For example, one $40 Kevlar pair may be able to hold something at seven hundred degrees Fahrenheit, while a more expensive pair can hold something twelve hundred degrees Fahrenheit. Kevlar allows the smith to hold things at temperatures higher than leather, and they do not shrink over time. However, there are two major drawbacks. Price is the first since a nice pair costs $100 or more.

Kevlar also rips and tears more easily than leather, so depending on what you're using them for, you may be disconcerted to notice holes appearing quickly. Kevlar excels when used in holding operations at high temperatures, but most blacksmiths on a budget do well with leather.

Respirators

Respirators are the fourth type of PPE commonly found in blacksmith shops, but they also fall below the must-have threshold *unless there is frequent use of grinders*. While grinding, respirators are as important as safety glasses. Those who doubt this advice are welcome to attend nearby blacksmithing events

3M full-face respirator

and listen in on conversations among older smiths. It soon becomes obvious that many of these smiths suffer from respiratory problems due to smoke and fine particles they have been exposed to. It boggles my mind how many people *still* don't believe in the use of respirators while grinding. It's almost as if the subject is taboo or that the jury is still out on whether or not fine particles damage the lungs. It should be obvious that fine particles from metal, wood, and synthetic materials—if they do not outright kill—certainly cause serious respiratory issues over time. ("Over time" again points out the similarity to hearing protection, another case of slow-acting, cumulative damage.) In fact, some smiths wear hearing protection but do *not* use respirators. Once again, imagine yourself sitting down to a discussion with your future self. Would you really prefer to have avoided hearing loss and nevertheless be OK with not being able to get a full breath of air at age sixty?

> **Liam's tip:**
> **Blow your nose after grinding. See black? Yeah, get a respirator.**

The 3M brand is the go-to for respirators (and most shop materials for that matter) and can be purchased for as little as forty or fifty dollars at your local hardware store. Different cartridges and filters are offered with respirators. These add-ons come with different colors on the side (yellow, black, blue, etc.). Google "3M respirator cartridge ratings" to easily identify which cartridges are used for what. The most common cartridges sold at hardware stores are yellow or pink, which indicate that the respirator filters organic vapors/acid gasses as well as fine particles since it comes with the particulate filter. The particulate filter is the *outside* filter and can be replaced frequently and easily at a low cost.

Half-face respirators are less expensive than full-face models but offer proportionately less protection. I've used both full-face and half-face versions (currently I am using a half-face respirator). Half face requires separate safety glasses, which are not needed with the full-face respirator. The full face is more than twice as expensive but comes with the added face protection. This can be nicely reassuring when operating a fast-moving grinder.

Dust Collection

Correct dust collection or extraction goes hand in hand with using a respirator. It can be toxic to leave particles floating in your shop space and difficult to vacuum everything each time you grind. Many dust-collection and dust-extraction options are available, including a simple eighteen-inch wall mount exhaust fan with shutters (which I currently use). This fan removes fine particles but primarily removes fumes and increases airflow. The fan can be bought online for around $200. Also hanging from my grinding room ceiling is a JET 1000CFM Air Filtration System that collects the finest airborne particles. Only by shining a bright light through the air can one see the particles that this machine collects. The important point is that whether you know it or not, very fine particles are constantly airborne in your shop, *and it's these virtually undetectable particles that damage your body the most.*

Wall mount exhaust fan

Larger pieces of material that can be easily seen will sink to the ground or be extracted by a dust-collection or dust-extraction unit. It's the ones you can't see that get you. The 1000CFM adds very important air filtration to your shop and is available online for around $380.

My third dust-removal system is a dust-extraction unit to collect particles directly under my belt grinder. This single, inexpensive unit only feeds to my grinder. It's a Shop Fox brand unit bought on Amazon.com, and with hoses, connections, hood, and air gate, the unit's total cost is just over $300. It works great if you want strong airflow heading to one machine. This unit was designed to collect dust in a bag; however, I have vented it straight outside for a few good reasons. Collecting dust in a bag takes up space and also brings up some fire safety concerns when you're grinding more than just wood on your grinder. In addition, I can create a slightly stronger airflow by venting straight outside and do not have to replace bags. Be sure to use flexible metal hoses rather than the plastic hoses that it comes with. Try to find hoses that have minimal ridges and are as smooth as possible on the inside. Heavily ridged hoses can inhibit airflow and cause particles to collect inside the hose.

Use a metal dust hood under your grinder rather than one made of plastic. Anything plastic in this setup is subject to melting and catching fire when exposed to steel sparks. When searching for a dust-extraction or dust-collection unit, keep in mind how many machines you want it to run to and how close to the machines you want to pull dust from. I have found that my small unit can work with two ports if necessary, but doing this cuts the suction power in half. While this can work, I prefer to have it dedicated to one grinder for a strong pull. The farther the unit is from the machine you want to pull dust from and the longer the hoses are, the less suction you will achieve. My extraction unit is located three feet from my grinder for easy access and maximum dust extraction.

Ergonomics

Ergonomics are another important aspect of safety in the shop. Working in a manner consistent with ergonomic principles protects your body over time. Thus, as with hearing and respirators, this is a PPE issue that seeks to counter long-term, cumulative, and sometimes not immediately obvious risks. Hammering is the number-one repetitive task engaged in by blacksmiths. It's therefore important to learn how to hammer properly and ergonomically to avoid the potential damage stemming from long hours spent hammering in the shop. Another boost from proper ergonomics is efficiency, both in terms of ratio of effort to output and in terms of greatly reduced downtime due to injuries. Improperly hammering thousands of times over years (or sometimes just months) can severely damage wrists, elbows, shoulders, or other joints. For example, the rotator cuff (which is supported by very small muscles) is at high risk for injuries such as tendonitis that arise from hammering and other repetitive tasks. The shoulder with all of its complex anatomy and functional versatility should almost be regarded as a distinct, highly valuable, and irreplaceable part of your shop's equipment. It follows that protecting the shoulder with the best ergonomic practices is essential to avoid injury.

> **Liam's tip:**
> **Photograph and video yourself working even if you don't plan on posting it online! Study your ergonomic practices from an outside perspective and adjust accordingly.**

Since many beginning blacksmiths may have preexisting injuries in the shoulder or elbow regions (for example, from high-school football and weightlifting), it's particularly important to adhere to ergonomics as you work with a hammer at the anvil. The hammer is supposed to be an extension of the arm. Correctly using a hammer will cause it to swing fluidly and to feel natural to you. The smith's grip on the hammer affects a lot of related systems, as does the smith's stance and distance from the anvil. Using a tight death grip on the hammer handle is asking for trouble.

Symptoms of poor ergonomics include your hands feeling weary at the end of the day and experiencing problems with your grip. When

Team striking with Shaun Williams

you hold the hammer handle too tightly, you're over stressing your hands as well as taking the direct shock from the impact of the hammer hitting the steel. Even though the steel is hot, it will still shock the hammer handle and cause vibrations that go into your hand and arm. These vibrations can destroy your joints. Ease up on the hammer handle to dissipate the stresses on your hands and other joints. The rebound of the anvil should also help with picking your hammer back up, and gripping the hammer loosely allows the rebound to properly pick the hammer up and continue working without strain.

There are a couple of advantages of a loose grip, such as the reduced strain on your body and allowing the anvil's rebound to help lift the hammer back up. If your hand and stance are rigid, then rebound can't work to your benefit, and you'll lose your flow and rhythm while you work. The blacksmith should also stand relatively close to the anvil while hammering. It is very common to see beginners take a stance too far away from the anvil, thereby overextending their arms in order to reach the anvil with their hammers. Luckily this is an easy fix and comes naturally over time once you become comfortable with the anvil and other tools. Bracing your feet properly allows your upper body to remain loose and relaxed.

If the smith's grip on the hammer handle is proper, he or she can forge for hours on end. In addition to simply holding the hammer loosely, three different common types of grips are used. The first is a closed-fist grip, which is most common for beginners. With the other two, the grip keeps the last two to three digits (middle, ring, and pinky fingers) off of the hammer handle, allowing the handle to pivot between index finger and thumb without obstruction from these last three digits. The second grip is where the hammer handle is pinched with the index and thumb on the sides of the handle. In the third type of grip, the hammer is held by the index and thumb, creating a ring shape with your fingers by enclosing the handle. Both of these latter grips allow the hammer to swing

First grip: loose closed fist

Second grip: pinched with index and thumb on sides of handle (my preferred grip)

Third grip; index and thumb encircle handle

and pivot, thereby greatly reducing the shock transferred to the hand.

The relation of the smith's arm to the distance of his or her body is also of great importance since it affects the angle of the elbow and shoulder when swinging a hammer. When you're forging, keep your elbow relatively close to your side instead of out to your right or left of your body. If your arm is out too far, you run the risk of damage to your body. The elbow should move but not greatly. The majority of your movement (and the velocity generated) should come from lifting the arm and hammer up with the legs, torso, and shoulder, and finally by quickly pivoting the hammer on the downswing in your loose handgrip. If the hammer can properly pivot in your hand, you free the range of motion necessary for your elbow. When you begin forging, your hammer control should be dealt with first and foremost. Without hammer control, your work is going to be difficult to complete since you'll neither be able to work for a long time nor be accurate in your use of a hammer. This is the first thing that a student is taught in my one-day basic blacksmithing class. Without it, all is for nothing. Aside from inefficient forging caused from poor hammer control and technique, it can also damage your body.

Approach the anvil by forming a sturdy stance close to the anvil base. Keep your hammer arm's elbow close to your side and form a loose grip on the hammer that allows you to pivot the hammer. When pivoting the hammer, it should almost look as if you're cracking a whip. Make a mental checklist of these ergonomic practices when you step up to the anvil, and over time they will become natural. I recommend recording yourself on video to study your technique from an outside perspective. I like to incorporate one key aspect of proper hammer control at a time, and once that aspect comes naturally, incorporate the next. It's important to do this early on in the game so that you aren't fighting deeply rooted bad habits down the road. As you hammer and work at the anvil, everything you do should look natural and fluid, not rigid and forced.

To recap, the key practices for proper hammer control are:

1. Proper stance at the anvil, starting with your feet. Work from the ground up.
2. Choosing and developing the correct grip out of the three accepted variations.
3. Keeping your elbow close to your side and using your entire body (legs, torso, and shoulder) to lift the hammer up and loosely crack it back down upon the hot steel.

Once these practices have become muscle memory, you can begin doing this with more speed and power.

Begin with a sturdy stance and body position to the anvil. Choose a proper grip on the handle.

Lift the hammer and arm up with your legs, torso, and shoulder in one fluid motion.

Power down with your torso. Maintain a loose grip and cock the hammer back.

"Crack the whip" in your loose grip as the hammer comes down, and allow the rebound of the anvil to pick the hammer back up. Repeat.

Lighting

In the forging area, it's beneficial to have dim lighting and an overall darker workspace in order to more accurately see the color of the steel you're working on. It's nearly impossible to judge how hot a piece of steel is in bright lighting. In grinding and finishing rooms, it should be just the opposite. Florescent or LED lights work well for overhead lighting and should be used liberally. For task lighting, I prefer an LED light, especially when I'm grinding. LED gives off a light that allows you to see scratch marks more easily on the grinder, marks that otherwise can't be seen except in direct sunlight.

> **Liam's tip:**
> **Position your overhead lighting so that there is always light in front of you. If your lighting hangs just slightly behind your head and work piece, you will create shadows.**

I hope that this short overview of blacksmithing PPE will encourage you to equip yourself in the shop properly. In the ideal situation, you will have and use all four primary PPE types and employ the best ergonomic practices. Take it into your own hands to provide yourself with proper PPE so that your blacksmithing career is not cut short because of injury or ill health.

How to teach yourself

In our culture, when faced with the challenge of learning something new, our first impulse is to go and find a teacher, a how-to book, or a YouTube instructional video. In blacksmithing as well, the traditional approach has been for the apprentice blacksmith to work under the close supervision of a master smith, slowly building his or her own skills while contributing to the latter's projects in a simple supporting role. In a similar way, would-be chefs often begin as line cooks tasked with prepping ingredients and assembling dishes in the kitchens of well-known chefs. The same pattern reoccurs in numerous other trades and crafts: carpentry, automotive maintenance, electrical work, plumbing, and so on.

But there are several problems with this traditional model in modern times. First, many—probably most—readers of this book are engaged in a day job or other demanding activities that prevent them from immersing themselves in a traditional blacksmithing operation. Second, blacksmithing is no longer the ubiquitous craft that it had been up until the turn of the twentieth century, so even finding a shop in which to be mentored as an apprentice would be quite difficult. Third, the emergence of blacksmithing as a hobby activity, supported by shows, competitions, Internet chat rooms, YouTube demonstrations, and so forth opens up new avenues for self-instruction. Accordingly, the focus of this book is not only how to start up your own blacksmith shop but also how to teach yourself the fundamental and even advanced skills of the blacksmithing craft.

Be aware and prepare yourself that learning on your own isn't easy. It will prove to be extremely time consuming, difficult, and at times frustrating. But this is by far the most rewarding method once a lesson is learned. One of my favorite parts of blacksmithing and knife making is overcoming an obstacle and learning a new skill by trial and error. That is true fulfillment that no one can hand to you. Once you get a taste of this, then you'll go back for more no matter how many times you fail. The content that you are reading in this book has been learned and developed through trial and error over countless thousands of hours and by using the self-teaching methods that are about to be covered.

Furthermore, advising the teach-oneself approach is a far cry from suggesting that anything goes. There's definitely a right and wrong way to go about building your skills by yourself. Being self-taught doesn't guarantee that you will end up with superior skills or that you will end up becoming a better smith than someone who was mentored by an experienced smith or took classes at blacksmithing events. If such classes or mentors are readily available near you and your schedule and financial resources permit taking advantage of them, then by all means do so. What follows, however, are suggestions that will help you to avoid the *wrong ways* of teaching yourself and ending up, after many hours of fruitless practice, with no improvement in your skills and potential injuries to your body.

GLOBAL VERSUS TARGETED PRACTICE

The following diagram summarizes a key approach to teaching yourself that I will term "targeted practice." At the heart of targeted practice lies a simple fact of arithmetic. Assume, as an example, that you want to develop skills at grinding a knife blade. One approach—let's call it "global practice"—would involve making, say, a total of fifty knives over the course of an entire year, during which time you would practice knife blade grinding once a

week. Targeted practice would suggest that if you want to master grinding blades, then get fifty simple knife blanks laser cut from a sheet of 3/16-inch mild steel and grind them all during one week. After grinding each blade, evaluate your weak points and then throw the blades away. Throwing away practice blades costs very little when using an inexpensive mild steel blank. In contrast, if you were working on a high-carbon steel blade that you had forged, throwing away even one blade after grinding errors would be far more costly in both time and money. If it takes you a year to forge and finish fifty knives, but only a week to grind fifty laser cut blanks, then you are essentially experiencing a year's worth of practice in one week. (See the "deliberate practice" discussion in *Talent Is Overrated*, by Geoffrey Colvin.) I believe this literature mischaracterizes the approach by calling it "*deliberate* practice." I would argue that all practice is deliberate, but that does not mean that it is either efficient or effective.

The theory behind targeted practice is elaborated in the previous diagram. Targeted practice entails working diligently on *a single step* in the process of an entire project rather than practicing on the project as a whole over and over. Top athletes have long utilized this approach, as exemplified by the prevalence of golf driving ranges, putting greens, tennis ball machines, and similar exercises that target very narrow rather than global skill sets. Targeted practice recognizes that in order to hone the skills involved in a whole process, skills first need to be broken down into individual steps, and then each of those steps needs to be targeted repetitively and deliberately.

The previous diagram also points out the challenges associated with targeted practice. It suggests that targeted practice is highly mentally demanding (highly physically demanding too) and can be not much fun. For example, throwing away fifty knife blades after practice during a week or two is probably not as rewarding as actually coming up with one or two finished knives. The finished knives, after all, can be shown to friends or family and given away as presents. It is relatively easy to ignore the fact that the two finished knives almost certainly exhibit serious flaws if examined by a master smith, who will examine them more closely and with more craftsmanship in mind than would your friends.

With grinding, forging whole knives, forging handles, or forging the tip of the blade, the specific focus of targeted practice depends on your and others' assessments of your current output. Maybe you struggle with forging the tips on your blades, so the best way of overcoming this difficulty is to set some time aside and practice working on forging tips of knives over and over on mild steel. This practice should—as figure 1 suggests—be designed to improve performance, and, to repeat, it will be not much fun. Nevertheless, the promise of targeted practice should always be kept in mind: you will gain more skill from this kind of practice focused on a specific, small subset of skills than you would by making a few knives from start to finish, one at a time. My friend Chris Williams uses this practice to teach his students and also uses these blanks to demo his Wilmont grinders at shows to potential customers. He takes a mild steel blank and lets the student or prospective buyer have at it. There is minimal cost incurred and maximum learning experienced gained.

Continuously Available Feedback

One element in the previous diagram might give the reader pause. It says that feedback is continuously available. If the emphasis in this book is on teach-yourself methods, how will feedback be available *at all*, never mind *continuously*? There is no fully satisfying answer to this question. If you do choose to teach yourself, and most importantly, if you find yourself working alone and isolated from other smiths, then your challenge is to fill in the feedback gap in as many separate, creative ways as possible. What follows are a few suggestions on how to do this.

Read It Backward

One trick that copy editors practice in their hunt for stray commas and word misspellings is to read the text they are copyediting *backward.* Reading backward forces the editor to slow way down. Second, reading backward endows each word with a certain strangeness or unfamiliarity, because the readers' expectations have been blocked by the backward progression. In an analogous manner, you may be able to take a project that you believe you have finished and "read it backward." Hold a knife by the blade and look back toward the handle, balance the project, change the lighting under which you examine it, look at it with one eye closed, and so on. The more you can do to make the familiar into the unfamiliar, the more likely you will find flaws in what you had just a few moments before thought to be "perfect." Every aspect of life and your work must be examined from multiple standpoints as each shows a different view.

Show Your Projects to Others

Even though having a mentor would mean that someone is actually watching you at work, you will be surprised to find that a master smith, by looking at your finished work, can see in it signs of the processes that went into its making without him or her being there. A friend of mine who likes to lift weights has as his chiropractor the former Mr. Olympia Franco Columbu. He reports that Columbu, just by looking at his musculature in his chiropractic office, can tell him what routines he has been doing at the gym and which parts of them are wrong. Bringing your projects to shows—even when you know they're not quite ready—is another avenue for opening up informed feedback. It is too easy to overlook mistakes when it is only your eyes on the material. Be sure to show your work to others.

EMBRACE THE SUCK

Another key aspect of teaching yourself is being able to be uncomfortable with the work you're making. You have to be willing to put yourself in unfamiliar situations and put in the hours necessary to be successful with this craft. I do my best to put myself in situations that will force me to push my skills to the limit. Let's say your friend wants you to make him a nice hunting knife for his birthday in two weeks, but you've never made a knife before. Why not start now? Go ahead and commit—if you want to

Homemade forge setup by young blacksmith Eric Chelstrom, practicing the mind-set discussed in this book. Get 'er done.

eventually make blades, that is. There is no better time than right now. That time limit and pressure to impress your friend will force you to progress leaps and bounds in a short amount of time.

If you just waited and waited and waited until one day at your leisure you started making knives, I guarantee you it would take at least twice as long to learn what you could have learned in a pressured situation. When I made my first sword in a time-constrained forty-five hours in the "Forged in Fire" competition, I quickly acquired numerous techniques, including a different handle construction, grinding a long blade, and unfamiliar finishing techniques. Learn to seek out projects and situations that will force creativity and to come up with solutions quickly.

> **Liam's tip:**
> **Go all in. Be willing to mess up.**

Constantly add projects to your schedule that will encompass a new technique to challenge you. It's all too easy to become complacent and comfortable in what you do, and that's when you know it needs to be switched up. At every BLADE Show, I try to challenge myself with unique knives and constructions, and most often I don't know exactly how it's done or how long it will take me to do it, but I know I need to do it and have it done properly in time for the show. So if someone isn't there to push you, you need to do it yourself by setting (even artificial) time limits or taking on more difficult projects. The most important rule of teaching yourself is never giving up. Although "never give up" sounds a little corny, it's the attitude you must have in order to improve in the workshop.

Some of the experiences I've faced by trial and error would include getting burned with hot steel by not understanding how long metal takes to cool down. I learned this one very early when I started, and unless by accident, I haven't made the mistake since. I learned that gripping my tongs too hard will cause my hands to be sore the next day, and I learned the hard way to properly hold hot steel with tongs to avoid my work piece from becoming airborne. All of these lessons are simple and fundamental, but they're the types of things that you'll be learning as you go. There are thousands of small lessons and personal nuances that develop over time.

KEEP A WORK JOURNAL

One of the struggles people have with overcoming obstacles or bad habits and techniques is not being aware of them in the first place. It's clear that you can't improve on something if you don't realize it needs to be improved upon. One trick is to be aware of what you're doing on a regular basis. Let's say you've been forging for three months now and are feeling pretty good with your progress and skill level. So go ahead and make an honest evaluation of your techniques and see what needs to change, because I can guarantee it can be improved. I'm eight years into my craft, and I'm constantly being challenged and reminded of how much I still need to learn. When you think you've conquered one thing, another comes to knock you to the ground and kick dirt in your face. Take regular photos of your work and time stamp them so that, looking back, you will see concrete evidence of the learning curve you have been traversing.

The majority of people aren't aware of their bad habits or the fundamentals lacking in their work. Today when I make a knife, I know what to look for, and I give myself an honest evaluation to the best of my ability. There is always something to improve upon, and you won't progress if you're not aware of what those things are. Look online at some skilled and experienced smiths whose work you admire. Take note of all the small details that make their work have integrity, and apply them to your work. Simply make an honest self-evaluation that will allow you to make the changes needed to improve yourself in the shop. This is admittedly difficult on your own because humans are inherently vain at times.

Sometimes you simply don't know what you don't know. Improving your work not only means knowing what it should be but also what it shouldn't be.

> **Liam's tip:**
> **See your mistakes that may be hiding by walking away from the material for one day to an entire week. Once you come back, it will be clear what's wrong.**

KEEP IT REAL

A lot of people ask, "How can I become a blacksmith without investing so much time?" There is no encouraging answer to this question. Like many things worth learning, you have to be willing to put in time to become skilled in blacksmithing. If you don't have at least several hours each week to dedicate to this craft, then perhaps It isn't the hobby or future business venture you thought you were signing up for. The key to becoming a "master" among your niche in any field is repetition using deliberate practice. It is this simple yet complex concept that is up to you to carry out. These practices aim to make this easier and clearer.

VIEW FAILURE AS A STEP UP, NOT DOWN

If you screw up a knife handle and then throw it away, see the failure as an opportunity to start over and improve upon your last one with the knowledge you gained from failing. I'm sure that there is something different you would do to the second handle that you learned from the first which can give you a better finished product in the end. Knowing what *not* to do is often better than knowing what *to* do in a sense. When I walk up to the anvil, I keep a mental list of things not to do when forging a taper; knowing things that don't work keeps me focused on the fundamentals that I do know.

> *Insanity is doing the same thing over and over again, but expecting different results.*
> *—Albert Einstein.*

If you keep making the same mistakes over and over (remember the work journal and project photos), then you won't move forward. Most often, failure allows me to create something far better than I would have if I hadn't previously failed. Knowing how to see failure as a step toward success—and not giving up—will separate you from the crowd. We should acknowledge the tendency on YouTube and Facebook for us and others to always put forth our best selves. When you see a legendary blacksmiths' project, always keep in mind that these projects are the tip of an iceberg and that underneath, hidden in the dark water, is an upside-down mountain of previous failures.

> *Success is not final, failure is not fatal: It is the courage to continue that counts.*
> *—Winston Churchill*

THE GOOD NEWS

The number-one best feeling that you get out of the workshop is overcoming a seemingly insurmountable challenge or figuring out how to solve an impossibly stubborn problem. *All* the projects you take on in the workshop are reducible to a series of problems to solve. The second-best feeling is holding a finished product that you're proud of. Teaching yourself is rewarding. It will undoubtedly take longer than learning from someone else, so be prepared for this. There is nothing wrong with learning from a mentor, and it has some obvious benefits, but it may also deprive you of habits, skills, and values that can only be taught from within.

When you start your journey, take these things into account. This approach will teach you lessons greater than those confined to the shop itself. It will teach you how to fail and how to turn seeming failure into success. It will teach you how to evaluate your own actions and continuously improve yourself small step by small step. It will teach you how to welcome challenges and work in uncomfortable situations that you may have otherwise avoided. Of everything in this book, it is this advice I wish I had been given when I started on my own learning curve nearly eight years ago. I hope that these principles can be applied to all aspects of your craft and life.

Afterword

It is likely that you have some remaining questions and reservations about entering into the craft's traditions of blacksmithing. The discussion of safety, in particular, might have been a bit daunting (it was meant to be), and the catalog of tools and the many decisions that you confront in building your own shop may seem almost too challenging. Therefore, I want to end this book with a few words of encouragement.

Blacksmithing is rightfully known as the king of all trades. And although blacksmiths are rarely found at the center of every town and village in America as they once were, blacksmithing has become part of a growing movement of those—especially among millennials—who want to discover for themselves and to recover for others sources of true value and authenticity. My friend explained to me that the other day around his house, he needed a stapler and quickly picked up one with which he was unfamiliar. He immediately noticed its heft, probably twice that of the current Office Depot varieties, and the effortless way in which it did its job. He realized that this unfamiliar stapler was at least thirty or forty years old. It had belonged to his grandfather, but now he will use it from this day forward. The old-fashioned stapler is a legacy tool, like half of the tools in my shop, many of which were made eighty to two hundred years ago. They work better than anything available at a big box store for $19.99. Like the stapler, these tools make you think, *Wow, I didn't even know things were ever made to work this well.* Blacksmithing offers you this sense of connection with an authentic past that will allow you to join with arts and crafts communities: artisanal bakeries, microbreweries, workshops turning out furniture made by hand, traditional quilting, and on and on.

Some fear that blacksmithing will ultimately die out and that its traditions will be lost. Quite the opposite is true. Blacksmithing is undergoing a huge revival, illustrated by the popularity of shows like "Forged in Fire" or, if you will, by the thousands of people who subscribe to blacksmithing and crafts related social media posts. I was recently speaking to an older friend of mine and fellow blacksmith, Paul Lundquist, who explained how the current day's blacksmiths are making progressions and innovations faster and in greater volume across the board than were being made in the blacksmithing revival that took place around the 1970s. He explained that this fact was due to the Internet and ease of learning among the online community of blacksmithing. More and more people are joining this trade every day and having fun with it. Hopefully this book can help you with that journey.

The history of blacksmithing was rooted in a highly decentralized system that led a young man first to serve (without pay) as an apprentice and then, after his skills were tested by a master smith, move on to a journeyman's status and so forth. This largely informal, decentralized system was replaced at the turn of the twentieth century with school-based vocational training and with the rise of the factory system in which each of many crafts and trades were deskilled. They were converted into manufacturing processes in which machines took over for skilled craftspeople and tradespeople. This was very ironic since it was blacksmiths who first forged the very tools that built the early machines that in turn became the foundation for the industrial revolution. This process of man-to-machine conversion continues today, although currently it is middle-class, white-collar workers whose careers are disappearing with the advent of artificial intelligence and machine learning. Fortunately, the job of a blacksmith can never be replaced by a machine because blacksmithing is also largely art, and machines are not capable of creating true art.

But while this trend continues, the cycle is also turning back on itself. The emergence of social media and YouTube has now made available to millions all over the world the sort of detailed, intimate connections that one hundred years ago were possible only between a master smith and his apprentice in an isolated workshop. The growing market for all manner of crafts and homemade products, and televised competitions like "Forged in Fire," has consolidated this phase in the history of smithing. These resources are now available to you, either to help in entering a full-time career or in engaging in a rewarding part-time hobby.

Although no one can provide you with all of the answers as you try to figure out this trade, there are many with whom you can share your experiences and who will help you significantly as you move along your learning curve. You will find that the blacksmithing community in general is comprised of very giving and helpful people. Although I consider myself to be largely self-taught, that means only that I work alone on a day-to-day basis and prefer to learn, and take enjoyment, from my mistakes in order to move forward. It certainly does not mean that I have not benefited from the generous help of many other smiths over the years. It is also reassuring that there is a wealth of distinct pathways into the craft, making it possible in the end for everyone to be able to take their own paths and develop unique styles.

Some of you will decide to forge chef's knives and swords that are defined in demanding ways by centuries of previous work; others will work in order to design and forge ornamental pieces and jewelry, products that have never before existed except in the blacksmith's imagination. The industrial revolution marked the beginning of the end of handmade, durable, high-quality products, and I think that we've begun to hit the threshold of tolerance for modern cheap alternatives. A push for quality is coming back after years of disposable plastic items in the marketplace.

Quality has *almost* been forgotten, and the standard of what we accept as quality has decreased so much that many (literally) don't know it could be better. I've seen it firsthand among people my age, and it's sort of shocking. Integrity and quality have gone out the window, to be replaced by volume and profits. I think that people are starting to wake up to this reality and to regain the respect and admiration for quality products that will last a lifetime and maybe even generations. I hope that you can take the information in this book to help you start blacksmithing and forging well-made items that in turn help spread awareness of what quality truly means.

The challenge ahead of us is not just about quality and durability. Most consumers, especially those my age (twenty-one), don't have any sort of understanding of how a given tool or household item should perform and last, and that ignorance has caused them to feel powerless inside a world of gadgets—yes, TV remotes but also the ignition system of a modern automobile—that pose unsolvable mysteries. Matthew Crawford, in *Shop Class as Soulcraft*, traces the implications of this disconnection between people and a world of things that they do not understand.

So the final message of this book is really quite simple: blacksmithing will take you along a path of growth and development that becomes deeper and richer every step of the way. It is a path that you ultimately must take on your own, but you will meet many helpful guides along the way, and you will quickly serve as a guide to others. Hopefully this book represents part of that help.

Good luck!

The author proudly holding a battle axe made in collaboration with Jason Lonon

Post online if you enjoyed the book! Use the hashtag #FORGEDthebook

Appendix

WORK JOURNAL

Project title/date:

_____

_____

Time to complete project:

_____

_____

Fundamental steps required?:

_____

_____

_____

What can be improved next time?:

_____

_____

_____

_____

_____

_____

_____

RESOURCES FOR BEGINNERS

ORGANIZATIONS AND SCHOOLS

ABS— www.americanbladesmith.com/

Abana— www.abana.org/

John C. Campbell Folk School- www.folkschool.org/

Penland School of Crafts— www.penland.org/

NESM— www.newenglandschoolofmetalwork.com/

Free Resources Offered by Individual Smiths

hoffmanblacksmithing.com

www.youtube.com/user/HoffmanBlacksmith96

@Hoffmanblacksmithing

Blade Forums— www.bladeforums.com/

Brian Brazeal— www.youtube.com/user/brianbrazealblacksmi

Nick Wheeler— www.youtube.com/user/NickWheeler33

Mark Aspery— www.youtube.com/user/MarkAspery

Brent Bailey— www.brentbaileyforge.com/

Kevin Cashen—http://cashenblades.com/mathertonforge/

Online Material and Tool Suppliers

General shop tools

Blacksmith Depot—
www.blacksmithsdepot.com/

Quick and Dirty Tools—
quickanddirtytools.com/

Anvils (New)

Nimba anvils— www.nimbaanvils.com/

Peddinghaus anvils—
www.peddinghausanvils.com/

Forges

Chile forge— www.chileforge.com/

NC Tool Co— www.nctoolco.com/products.php?cat=Gas+Forges

Grinders

Grizzly— www.grizzly.com/

Wilmont grinders— www.wilmontgrinders.com/Pages/default.aspx

Wuertz grinders—www.traviswuertz.com/

Abrasives

Tru Grit Abrasives—https://trugrit.com/

Super Grit Abrasives— www.supergrit.com/

Blade Steel and Material Supply

Alpha Knife Supply— www.alphaknifesupply.com/shop/

Masecraft Supply Co—http://masecraftsupply-com.3dcartstores.com/

Kelly Cupples Steel—(e-mail) Octihunter@charter.net

Online Metals— www.onlinemetals.com

Definitions

Anvil—Heavy, dense surface on which to hammer and shape metal

Clinker—Hard, glassy conglomerate of impurities burned from coal

Damascus steel—Modern-day term for welding multiple layers of different steels together

Dies—Faces of striking or pressing implements such as a hammer face or peen during forging processes

Fire pot—Part of the forge that contains the fire

Forge—Heat source for metal: can be wood, charcoal, coal, propane, or electric

Forge welding—Welding two pieces of steel together using traditional methods in a forge

Forging—The act of blacksmithing and shaping metal, also called smithing

Forging hammer—An extension of the smith's dominant arm, used to impact and move metal *via* the force of your body

Fullering—Displacing material in a specific and controlled direction using fullers

Hammer eye—Open area in a hammer for the handle

Hardy hole—Square hole in a traditional anvil used for extra tooling

Holdfast—Pritchel hole tool used to clamp work in place on the anvil

Hot cuts—Hardy tool used as a chisel to cut hot steel in half

Hydraulic forging press—Hydraulic machine designed to replace the work of a hand hammer on steel

Iron—Natural element mined from the earth: ingredient in steel and much softer than steel

Power hammer—Heavy hammer powered by air or electricity to replace the work of manually hammering steel

PPE—Personal protective equipment

Pritchel hole—Round hole in a traditional anvil used for extra tooling and punching

Quenching medium—Liquid in which hot steel is quenched during the hardening process: can be oil, water, or air

Quenching tank—Metal container used to hold large volumes of liquid quenching medium

Rebound—The bounce of your hammer after contacting the face of your anvil

Scale—Black oxidation formed after steel turns red hot

Slack tub—Water cooling bucket for hot steel

Spring swage—Hardy tool used to form different patterns and shapes using top and bottom spring dies

Steel—Manmade material using a mix of iron and carbon

Tongs—Used to hold and turn metal too hot to touch with bare hands

Tuyere—Air source and ash collection area for coal forges

Wrought iron—Impure manmade iron alloy with silica and slag

Book References

Shop Class as Soulcraft - by Matthew Crawford

Talent is Overrated: What Really Separates World-Class Performers from Everybody Else - by Geoff Colvin

About the Author

In the summer of 2008 I was 13 years old, anxiously waiting to become an eighth grader and bored out of my mind one evening in the mountains of Appalachia. Without permission from my dad (I quickly learned that acting first and asking for forgiveness later has it's benefits) I found a piece of aluminum suitable for smashing. A small stick fire was built and the aluminum started taking shape with the help of an old framing hammer.

I soon discovered the wonder in flattening and shaping metal that would forever change the direction of my future. A few hours later, this time with the help of my father, we dug out a massive pit in the ground to build a larger wood fire in which I used to heat up my first piece of glowing red steel. I learned quickly how to use tongs....

I had already caught the bug, so we gathered and scrounged for the essential tools from around the house to start forging immediately.

When I get a new idea or itch to do something, I have a tendency to do it right away, even if it means I don't have the optimum set up. These keystone tools that went to build my future career would be the anvil, tongs, and hammer. The anvil used was an old ball hitch, hardly your best case scenario, but this weighed around 10 pounds and had a solid enough surface to hammer steel on. The tongs were vise grips reluctantly surrendered from my father's tool box, and the hammer was an old claw framing hammer. Doesn't sound too luxurious does it? Well I thought it was!

All of this was expeditiously gathered and underway in one evening, without leaving the house. In the same day I went from becoming a bored 13 year-old to a fascinated up and coming blacksmith. All of this evolved into the current business and passion I have today. At the age of 19 I was fortunate enough to purchase a beautiful 10 acre plot of land outside of Boone, NC for the future site of Hoffman Blacksmithing to be constructed in spring of 2018. I've been able to teach private lessons to students from as far away as Australia, and create a career I wouldn't have dreamed of when I started. Today, in the year 2017, I specialize in hand forged axes with the help of my team. Currently I'm 21 years old and excited to have bigger and better plans for the years to come, growing and transforming my craft and business.

Made in the USA
San Bernardino, CA
27 December 2017